Ever Heard of

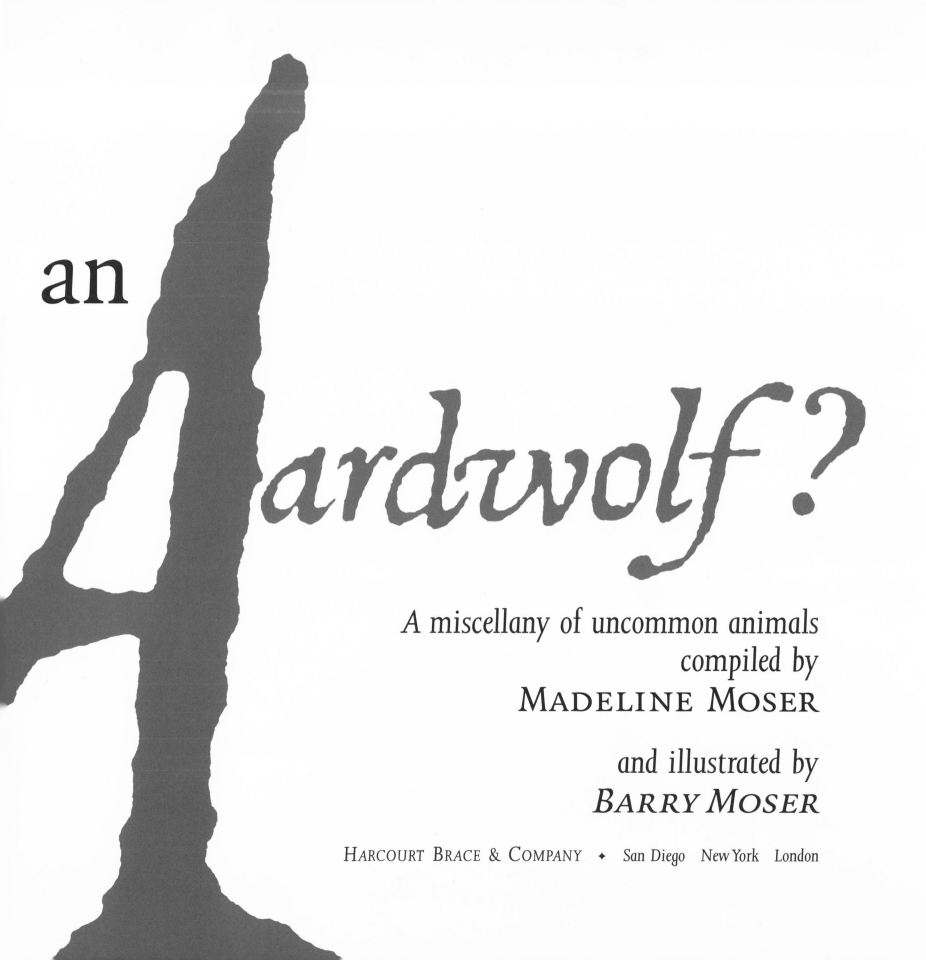

an Aardwolf?

A miscellany of uncommon animals
compiled by
MADELINE MOSER

and illustrated by
BARRY MOSER

HARCOURT BRACE & COMPANY ✦ San Diego New York London

Library of Congress Cataloging-in-Publication Data
Moser, Madeline.
Ever heard of an aardwolf?/by Madeline Moser;
engravings by Barry Moser.—1st ed.
p.   cm.
Summary: Presents information about twenty animals with unusual
names and habits, including the loris, okapi, viscacha, and zorilla.
ISBN 0-15-200474-2
1. Animals—Miscellanea—Juvenile literature.
[1. Animals—Miscellanea.] I. Moser, Barry, ill. II. Title.
QL49.M825   1996
599—dc20   95-37878

First edition
F E D C B A

Printed in Singapore

For my best friend and greatest love,
my husband Dan
—M. M.

And for my friend
Vance Studley
—B. M.

Ever heard of an aardwolf? (say: ARD-wulf)

The aardwolf is not really a wolf at all. It's a member of the hyena family and lives in Africa. Though it's a meat eater, like wolves and hyenas, it has to be satisfied with termites and insects because its jaws are weak and its teeth are small and widely spaced.

How about a vicuña? (say: vi-KOON-yuh)

The vicuña is a member of the camel family, and lives up above the tree line in the Andes Mountains of South America. Vicuñas have extralarge hearts to pump the great quantity of blood that is needed to provide enough oxygen to live at such high elevations.

Or a loris? (say: LOR-us)

Lorises live deep in the tropical forests of southern Asia. They spend
most of their time in trees, where they climb so slowly and carefully
that they don't even rustle the leaves. But their speed is lightning quick
when they are hunting the lizards and insects they like to eat.

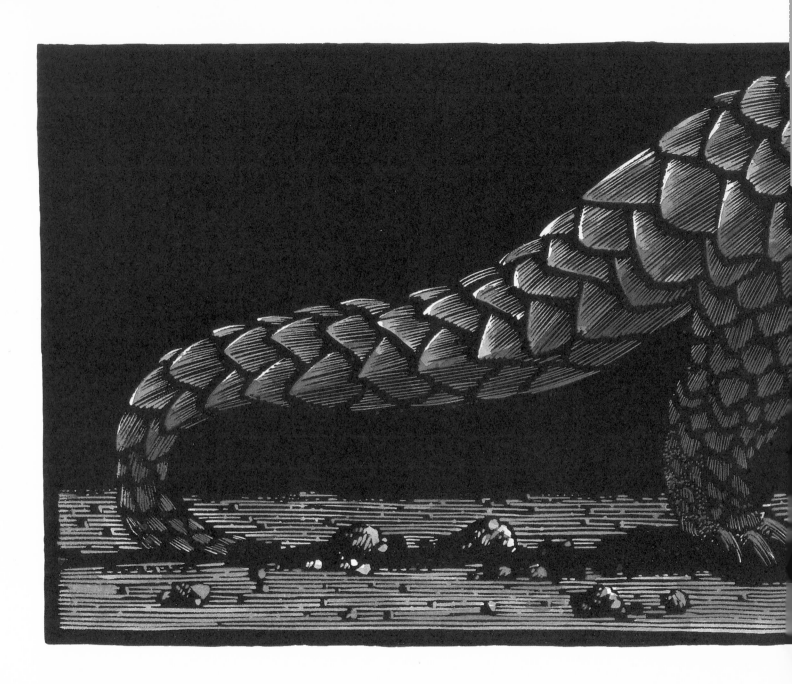

Or a pangolin? (say: PAN-ga-lin)

The pangolin looks like a large reptile, but it is actually an African-Asian mammal. It has no teeth at all, so it swallows insects whole. It eats small rocks and pebbles, too. The rocks and pebbles stay in the pangolin's stomach to grind up its food.

Ever seen a viscacha? (say: vis-KAH-chuh)

Viscachas are curly tailed, rabbitlike rodents that live in large burrows that they often share with other animals such as snakes, toads, and foxes. Viscachas collect items like bones, rocks, trash, and jewelry to place on top of their burrows.

Ever heard of a naked mole rat? (say: NAY-kid MOWL rat)

The naked mole rat has almost no hair and lives in a maze of tunnels
that it digs in the ground with its big front teeth. Its lips close
behind these teeth, which helps to keep dirt from getting into its
mouth. It's easy to see why naked mole rats rarely go above ground.

Or a horseshoe bat? (say: HOR-shew BAT)

There are more than sixty different kinds of horseshoe bats living in *Asia*, *Africa*, *Australia*, and *Europe*. They are only about three inches long, with a twelve-inch wingspan, and they can hover in midair like hummingbirds. They get their name from the horseshoe shape of their noses.

Ever seen an okapi? (say: oh-KAH-pee)

The shy okapi lives in the tropical forests of Africa. It is a relative of the giraffe, and it has a tongue so long that it can reach around and lick the corners of its own eyes! Okapis use their strong tongues to grasp branches and pull off the leaves they like to eat.

Or a proboscis monkey? (say: pruh-BAH-sus MUNG-kee)

The male proboscis monkey uses his nose like a horn to make loud calls
to other monkeys in his group. His nose grows throughout his life, and
when he is old he is likely to have a nose so large that he has to hold it
aside in order to eat. Females' noses are small and stubby.

Or a solenodon? (say: so-LEEN-uh-don)

Solenodons are found only on certain islands of the West Indies. They have very long, flexible, rubbery noses that they use to feel about the little spaces where they might find the food they like—insects, worms, small reptiles, frogs, and birds. They hunt at night.

Have you met a platypus? (say: PLA-ti-pus)

The platypus is a very unusual mammal. It has webbed feet and a
ducklike bill, and it does not give birth to live young, as other
mammals do. It lays eggs. And it has ribs in its neck, like a snake!
The platypus lives in Tasmania and eastern Australia.

Or a bush dog? (say: BUSH dawg)

The bush dog doesn't look like most other dogs, and it is sometimes called a vinegar fox, but it is a real dog. Its feet are webbed, and it is such a good swimmer that it often hunts fish and frogs in and under the water. Bush dogs live in Central and South America.

Or a bush baby? (say: BUSH BAY-bee)

Bush babies have huge eyes that help them see well enough in the dark
to hunt at night. Bush babies hear well, too, but when they sleep, they
fold their ears closed just as you would fold up a paper fan. They live in
the forest or the African bush, and their cry sounds like a human baby's.

Ever heard of a babirusa? (say: bob-uh-ROO-suh)

The babirusa is a wild hog found on the islands of Indonesia. Males have four tusks that grow from their snouts. The upper tusks seem to have no purpose other than beauty. Babirusas like to dine out, and sometimes they swim from island to island to feast on new supplies of water plants and fruit.

How about a uakari? (say: wah-KAH-ree)

The uakari is the only monkey of South and Central America that does not have a long tail. Its coat is shaggy, but its face is red and bald. When it spends time in the sun, its face becomes a bright red. But if it lives in the shade, its face turns pale pink.

Or an emperor tamarin? (say: EM-pur-ur TAM-uh-run)

Emperor tamarins are squirrel-sized monkeys that live in the lowland rain forests of Peru, Bolivia, and Brazil. They were named by nineteenth-century explorers, who thought that the tamarins' elegant mustaches made them look like Emperor William II.

Ever seen a zorilla? (say: zuh–RIL–uh)

Zorillas, relatives of the skunk, live in Africa. When they are threatened, they fluff up their fur to look large. If that doesn't scare off the attacker, the zorilla screams, lifts its tail, and sprays the animal with a foul, stinky fluid. The smell is so bad that the attacker often passes out.

How about a zebu? (say: ZEE-boo)

The zebu, like other cows, is sacred to the followers of the Hindu religion.
A Hindu will not kill or even restrain these animals. They roam freely about
in the cities and towns and often pick and choose food items from the
stands of outdoor markets.

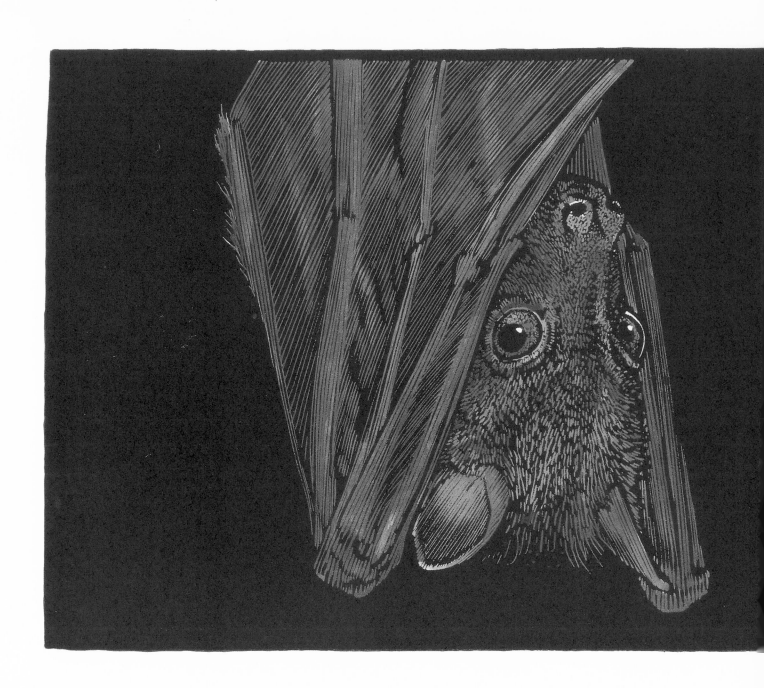

Or a flying fox? (say: FLY-ing FOX)

Flying foxes eat only fruits and flowers. They are not really foxes.
They are large bats with doglike faces. Often they hang from trees
with one foot and eat with the other. Hanging from branches, they
sometimes look like pieces of fruit themselves.

Ever heard of a horse? (say: HORS)

Of course!!!

And we can tell you more....

The Aardwolf

The aardwolf is a member of the hyena family and lives in the plains and open woodlands of eastern and southern Africa. It weighs between fifteen and thirty-one pounds and feeds primarily on termites, which it hunts at night. The aardwolf's keen hearing helps it locate termites, and its long, sticky tongue licks them right up.

Most hyenas have strong teeth and jaws and can eat and digest flesh and bone, but the aardwolf's stubby molars can't chew meat and its jaws are too weak to eat anything other than bugs.

Aardwolves are also unlike members of the hyena family in that they forage alone.

Aardwolves live in their own burrows or in dens abandoned by other animals. On sunny days they spend most of the morning lying outside, but when it's rainy they might stay in their dens the entire day.

Females give birth to a litter of two to four pups after a three-month pregnancy.

The Vicuña

Weighing about one hundred pounds, the vicuña is the smallest member of the camel family. Through the years vicuñas have been hunted for their fur, which was considered by some people to be more precious than many gems. The entire vicuña population was very nearly wiped out.

Vicuñas live on the high plateaus of the Andes Mountains, above the tree line but below the snow line, and always near a good supply of water. Living at such high elevations is difficult because there is less oxygen in the air. The vicuña has developed an unusually large heart to pump more oxygen-rich blood to all the parts of its body.

The open and hilly terrain of the Andes plateaus is covered with the short, tough, grasslike plants that are the vicuña's food. These plants are so tough that they can wear down teeth. Luckily, vicuñas' teeth grow continuously throughout their lives.

The Loris

The loris is a primate that lives in southern India and Southeast Asia. It weighs between eight ounces and four pounds and has short limbs and a short, stubby tail. Lorises' powerful hands and feet hold on to branches as they climb slowly and deliberately throughout the trees. They move so slowly that they can go unnoticed by enemies and prey. Sometimes when lorises want to play, cool off, or have a snack, they will hang by their feet so that their arms are free.

Usually lorises hunt for insects, but they eat lizards and fruit as well. They hunt at night and during the day sleep curled up like balls in the hollows of trees. Lorises live alone for the most part, but sometimes females will nest together.

The Pangolin

Pangolins are the only mammals covered with scales. The scales are made of the same material that forms horns in some other animals.

There are four species of African pangolins and three species of Asian pangolins. Only Asian pangolins have external ears.

Some species of pangolins rest in burrows in the ground and others stay in trees, but they all live and hunt on their own. When it needs to protect itself, the pangolin curls up

into a ball; its scales are so hard that most predators can't penetrate them. It also uses its tail like a whip. The scales on a pangolin's tail can cause severe damage to the flesh of other animals. The tail is also prehensile in some pangolins and can grip things like branches, so they are often found hanging upside down in trees.

Pangolins have no teeth. Instead, they have long, sticky tongues that curl up in their mouths. When they need to catch a meal, they unroll their sticky tongues and then retract them covered in termites or ants, which they swallow whole.

The Viscacha

There are two kinds of viscachas, both of which live in South America. One, the mountain viscacha, lives high in the Andes Mountains; the other, the plains viscacha, is found in the lower grasslands.

Mountain viscachas live in colonies of hundreds of individuals. They spend their days feeding on grasses and plants

and basking in the sun. When a viscacha becomes alarmed or frightened, it warns the others with a whistling call. Unlike most rodents, mountain viscachas do not live in burrows, preferring to find shelter among the rocks.

Plains viscachas do live in burrows. They are crepuscular animals: they search for their meals of grasses and plants at dawn and dusk. They collect different kinds of odd objects, such as bone, rocks, or trash, to carry home with them and place on top of their burrows.

Like rabbits and other rodents, the viscacha has front teeth that grow continuously throughout the animal's life. The teeth don't grow too long because the viscacha is constantly gnawing on things like sticks and roots.

The Naked Mole Rat

Naked mole rats are considered naked because they have so little hair that they don't appear to have any at all. This might help them to keep cool in the tunnels they dig in the dry, warm soil of the East African savannas where they live. They very rarely go above ground and are therefore pale as well as naked.

They are social animals that work together, just as bees and other insects do. Like bees, they have a hierarchy within their colony that consists of workers and nonworkers. Workers are smaller than nonworkers and are responsible for digging tunnels, finding food, and bringing it back to the nest to share with the nonworkers.

There is only one breeding female in every colony, and it is the nonworkers' duty to nest with her. Though nonworkers are usually female, they can't reproduce unless something happens to the breeding female that prevents her from bearing more offspring. If this occurs, one of the nonworkers can replace her.

The Horseshoe Bat

Horseshoe bats live in Asia, Africa, Australia, and Europe. They grow to be about three inches long, with twelve-inch wingspans, and they fly slowly and gracefully. Early Europeans thought that these bats were vampires. Farmers observed them hovering over animals in barns and assumed the bats were feeding on the animals' blood. Actually, the bats are there to catch the insects the animals attract.

The horseshoe-shaped nose plays an important role in echolocation. Through its nostrils, a bat emits ultrasonic sounds, sounds so high pitched that humans can't hear them. These sounds bounce off objects, creating echoes that help the bat determine where things are. Since bats travel and hunt at night, and have small, inefficient eyes, this is their way of "seeing in the dark."

Horseshoe bats spend their days wrapped in their wings, roosting in the hollows of caves, mines, dens, and even the attics of houses.

The Okapi

The okapi is a large, shy animal found in the rain forests of Zaire. Its brown coat matches the color of the rotting leaves on the forest floor, and the stripes on its back end blend with shadows and splashes of light. The okapi's camouflage is so effective that even from as close as eighty feet, it can't be seen in its native habitat.

Okapis are active during the day, traveling along systems of clear paths in the forest. For the most part they eat leaves that they pull off trees with their long, blue-black tongues. Their tongues are so long that they can lick and wash almost any area of their own bodies. Okapis also eat buds, tender shoots, fruit, grass, ferns, fungi, red clay, and even the charcoal from burned trees.

We don't know much about okapis because their camouflage and shy nature keep them hidden from man.

The Proboscis Monkey

Proboscis monkeys live in troops of about twenty individuals, in swamps and near rivers in the coastal forests of Borneo. They are Old World monkeys, which are the species of monkeys commonly found in Asia, Africa, and Europe. New World monkeys are native to Central and South America.

The male proboscis monkey's nose grows continuously throughout his life and is used like a loudspeaker. He can make very loud calls that echo over the swamps, ensuring

that the other monkeys can hear him wherever they are. When a call is made, his nose swells up like a balloon. It also swells up and turns red when the monkey gets angry or excited. The female has a smaller nose that stops growing when she reaches maturity. Females have bodies about half the size of the males', which weigh up to fifty-two pounds. Proboscis monkeys eat leaves and mangrove shoots. They like to swim and have often been observed doing something like the doggie paddle.

The Solenodon

Solenodons weigh about two pounds and live in the forests of the West Indies, where there is plenty of ground cover to keep them well hidden. They are solitary animals, living alone throughout most of their lives, except when they mate or when they are young and live with their mothers.

Since solenodons hunt at night, they must be able to listen for and smell potential meals. The nose is an all-

important tool for the solenodon. It is long and very flexible, and it can move in all directions, like a long, hairy probe. This benefits the solenodon by allowing it to find food in the cracks and crevices of rocks and trees, and in all the hidden locations that are inaccessible to animals with less gifted noses. When prey is located, solenodons quickly bite it and inject a venomous saliva, which paralyzes the prey and makes it easy to eat.

The Platypus

When the platypus was discovered by English explorers around 1798, they could not believe it was real. It had features of mammals, birds, and reptiles, and was unlike any animal they had ever seen.

The platypus is a monotreme, meaning that it uses only one body opening to expel the products of its reproduc-

tive, digestive, and urinary systems. Humans, by comparison, use three.

It also has webbed feet, which are useful since it is often in the water searching for food. When swimming, the platypus paddles with its two front feet and uses the back feet for steering. A flap of skin involuntarily covers the animal's eyes and ears when it goes underwater, so the platypus relies on its sensitive, ducklike bill to navigate.

When a female platypus is ready to lay her eggs, she digs a burrow in the bank of a river or lake that meanders along the ground for thirty-five feet or more. After laying her eggs, she stays in the burrow about ten days to hatch them.

The platypus, like the solenodon, is one of the few venomous mammals. The male has clawlike spurs on the heels of his hind legs. Poison is emitted when the spurs are kicked into another animal.

The Bush Dog

The bush dog, also known as the vinegar fox, is a very elusive creature that lives in Central and South America.

Because bush dogs are so rarely seen, very little is known about them or about their habits.

Bush dogs are excellent swimmers. Their feet are webbed, which helps them hunt for fish and frogs in the water, but they can hunt on land as well. When they do, they usually travel in packs of ten or more. Bush dogs have been known to prey on animals that are much larger than they are. For instance, though bush dogs weigh only eleven to fifteen pounds, they have been seen hunting capybaras—large, rodentlike animals that weigh approximately one hundred pounds.

Only one dominant female in a pack appears to be capable of reproducing. She might have two litters of two to six pups each year.

The Bush Baby

The bush baby got its name because it often lives in the open shrubby regions of Africa, which are called the bush, and because its call sounds just like the cry of a human baby.

Bush babies are arboreal primates—they spend most of their time in trees. They are active at night, hunting for good things to eat, like tree gum, small birds, lizards, insects, and fruit. Their enormous eyes help them to see in the dark and, along with their excellent hearing, to locate prey and be aware of predators. During the day they rest, sleeping in nests made of leaves and sticks or in the hollows of trees. They also like to huddle up together and doze on wide branches.

Bush babies can leap from tree to tree, using their powerful hind legs to catapult them off a branch. When they're on the ground, they hop like kangaroos. Depending on the species, bush babies range in size from less than two ounces to nearly four pounds.

The Babirusa

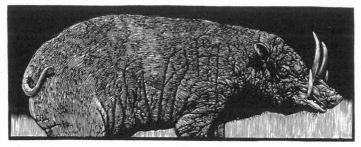

The babirusa is a relative of the pig. Indonesian natives thought that its tusks looked like deer antlers, so they named the animal "babirusa," which means "pig-deer." Adult babirusas can weigh as much as 220 pounds and can grow to be over three feet tall. Some have wrinkly skin, others have smooth. But either way, they enjoy spending their days covered with mud, which is plentiful near the edges of rivers and lakes in the moist forests where they live. After a hard day rolling in the mud, babirusas head out at night to forage for water plants, leaves, fruit, fungi, and insect larvae. They depend on their keen hearing to get around safely in the dark.

Only male babirusas have tusks. The lower tusks are used for fighting, but the upper tusks appear to be a decoration that makes them more attractive to females. Females have five-month pregnancies and typically give birth to one or two "babiruslets."

The Uakari

The uakari has hardly any fat beneath its facial skin, making it look gaunt or starved. The uakari has a tail that is just six to seven inches long. It is the only monkey in South America that does not have a full tail. Normally, New World monkeys have prehensile tails, about the same length as their heads and bodies together. The uakari's tail is not only short, it is shaggy, like the rest of its body. This shaggy coat makes the uakari look much larger than it really is; underneath all that fur it is long and slender.

Uakaris live together in large, peaceful groups, eating leaves, seeds, fruits, and buds. They live in the trees in and around the swamp forests of the Amazon Basin. When they want to rest they stay high up in the trees, but when it's time to go somewhere, they climb down and travel through the lower branches, leaping as much as twenty feet from tree to tree.

The Emperor Tamarin

Emperor tamarins are New World monkeys that live in the lowland forests of Peru, Bolivia, and Brazil. They are about the size of squirrels, which makes them one of the smallest  of the true monkeys. They are diurnal, or active during the day, and omnivorous, meaning that they will and can eat anything—although they prefer fruits and insects. They are sensitive to strong sunlight and therefore spend most of the hot part of the day in the deepest and densest part of the forest.

Grooming is an important part of the tamarins' social lives; they even like to clean each other's teeth. They use a variety of facial expressions to communicate.

Tamarins mate for life and live in very harmonious groups of two to ten individuals. They are usually born as twins. Fathers assist in the birth of the young and often carry them on their backs. All the members of a group share the responsibility of bringing up the young ones. It is a community activity.

The Zorilla

Zorillas weigh between one and three pounds and live in many parts of Africa, where they hunt for insects, small mammals, snakes, and birds. They hunt at night and rest during the day in shelters among the rocks or in shallow burrows.

The zorilla is also known as the African polecat. It has a thick black coat with white stripes, which makes it look like

its relative the skunk. Like the skunk, the zorilla has scent glands below its tail. These glands produce a fluid that has a very offensive odor and is used to scare off or even knock out predators. Before spraying, the zorilla will fluff up its fur as a warning and intimidation tactic. If the warning doesn't succeed in scaring off the enemy, the zorilla raises its tail and screams. Then it sprays. In the most frightening and dangerous situations, the zorilla will just fall over and play dead. Smelly dead.

The Zebu

The zebu is easily distinguished from other cattle because it has a great hump on its shoulders and a large flap of skin that hangs from its throat. The flap of skin, called a dewlap, can get so long that it actually touches the ground.

Zebus, along with all cattle, are considered sacred by members of the Hindu religion, who allow zebus to come and go as they please in their towns and cities. Non-Hindus, however, have used the zebu as a worker to pull plows and turn gristmills. They also keep it for its milk. Because zebus tolerate hot weather easily, they have been exported from their native range in India and Africa to other areas with hot climates, where most types of cattle do not fare well.

The Flying Fox

Flying foxes are large bats that live in Australia, Asia, and Africa. During the day they roost with hundreds of other flying foxes, hanging from trees or the faces of cliffs, all wrapped up in their wings, which keeps them warm and protects them from the elements. When they get too hot, they drool on themselves, open their wings, and flap to

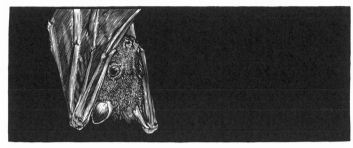

create a cooling fan. At dusk they fly off to look for food and will travel many miles in their search. Because they are so large—about the size of a small dog—and have broad wing-spans of up to five feet, during flight they can beat their wings slowly and glide.

There are nearly a thousand kinds of bats, and they make up almost one-quarter of all the mammalian species known.

Recent scientific research suggests that flying foxes may actually be primates, which would mean that they are more closely related to monkeys and humans than they are to rodents.

The Horse

Of course! You know the horse. Man has known horses for a long time; images of the horse even appear in prehistoric cave paintings.

But did you know that horses were not always the friend and servant of people we know them to be today? There was

a time when men hunted horses with spears and bows and arrows. They even stampeded herds of horses over the edges of cliffs to kill them. Then they'd skin and eat them.

Horses have also been important in our myths and legends. Think of the elusive horned unicorn and the centaurs, whose human trunk stems from a horse's body; and remember noble, winged Pegasus bearing his young rider, Bellerophon, up to the heavens.

Even animals as well known as the horse can surprise us.

The illustrations in this book were engraved in Resingrave, a synthetic wood engraving medium invented by Richard Woodman of Redwood City, California. The black-and-white proofs of the printed blocks were enlarged on a laser scanner, hand-colored by the artist using transparent watercolor, and then reduced to fit the book's design.

The type is Joanna and Joanna Italic, designed by the preeminent British designer, typographer, and sculptor Eric Gill. The design was named after his daughter, Joanna Gill Hague, and was first shown in 1930 at Gill's own private press, Gill & Hague, in Piggotts, Buckinghamshire, England.

The lettering on the title page and dust jacket is the work of Judythe Sieck and is based on the letterforms of the sixteenth-century Spanish writing master Francesco Lucas as found in the Arte de Escrevir de Francisco Lucas of 1580.

The book was designed by Barry Moser and Judythe Sieck. The paper is Mohawk Superfine. Separations were made by Bright Arts, Ltd., Singapore. The printing was done by Tien Wah Press, Singapore, under the direction of Warren Wallerstein and Stan Redfern.